Sad Jazz:

Sonnets

Sad Jazz:

Sonnets

Tony Barnstone

THE SHEEP MEADOW PRESS
RIVERDALE-ON-HUDSON, NY

All inquiries and permission requests should be addressed to:
The Sheep Meadow Press
P.O. Box 1345
Riverdale-on-Hudson, NY 10471

Designed and typeset by The Sheep Meadow Press.
Distributed by The University Press of New England.

Printed on acid-free paper in the United States. This book meets the guidelines
for permanence and durability of the Committee on
Production Guidelines for Book Longevity of the Council on Library
Resources.

Library of Congress Cataloging-in-Publication Data

Barnstone, Tony.
Sad jazz : sonnets / Tony Barnstone.
p. cm.
ISBN 1-931357-27-7 (alk. paper)
1. Sonnets, American. I. Title.

PS3552.A7215S23 2005
811'.54--dc22

2005018187

This book is for my mother,

Elli Tzalopoulou Barnstone

CONTENTS

Acknowledgments

The Bed

Petrarch: Sonnet 196   2

Marriage Psalm   4
Dancing out of the Shower   5
Kabbalah   6
It   7
Falling Through   8
In Her Dream He Touches Her Shoulder   9
In a Hotel in Portugal   10
At Suicide Beach   11
How To Live in This World   12
Throwing Stones at the Beach   13
And the Sea Takes Their Wishes   14

Thing in the Mirror

Dark Lord   16
Insect Wings   17
Zombies   18
Thing in the Mirror   19
Nightmare Kiss   20
The Grave   21
Spider Woman   22
Spider Man   23
The Orchid Creature   24
He Pays the Bill at the Sidewalk Café   25

The Happiest Man in the World

The Audit   28
The Happiest Man in the World   29
He Gets Up off the Floor   30
She Settled for Him   31
His Younger Wife   32
They Had Terrific Sex   33
He Goes to See the Doctor   34
After Eighteen Years   35

What She Said

Petrarch: Sonnet 195   38

Break up with Him (A How-to Manual)   40
Another Troy   41
The Hook   42
Antonyms   43
What She Said   44
What He Heard   45
What He Tries Not to Say   46
What Her Father Said   47
Laughing Poem   48
Screw the Beatles   49
A Bowl of Bean Soup   50

Driving Away from Her

Bad Drivers   52
After She Sat Down on the Couch and Told Him the
    Marriage Was Done   53

The Pits   54
His Wheels Are Whining   55
Suicide Road   56
He Saw Her Car   57

Aftermath

A Children's Tale   60
Until She Left   61
Out, Out, Out   62
Zero at the Bone   63
The Bed Is Wide   64
George Harrison Died around the Same Time
    His Marriage Did   65
He Wishes He Were Dead   66
Sad Jazz   67
On a Blow-Up Bed in the Study of His Father's Apartment 68
Cut Off   69
Insects   70
Wet Paper   71
The Ghost Limb   72
Barbeque   73
Aftermath   74

End of the Vacation

Two Tickets   76
His Niece and Nephew on the Beach   77

Drinking Cuervo Gold with Andy, Joe and Roman and a Guy from
    Liverpool Named Sven at Roman's Bar in Serifos, Greece 78
Heart Sushi   79
Waking Up Drunk   80
In These Old European Towns the Streets Wrap Back upon

Themselves Like an Insidious Argument 81

After the Night Swim 82

Foxes 83

In the Ghetto 84

Bright Surface Seen through a Train Window 85

The Truth Is He Never Was Good at Flirting, But His Friends
    Did Their Best to Set Him Up 86

A Cathedral in San Gimignano 87

End of the Vacation 88

Get Zen

He Murders His Darlings 90

Like a Man in a Cubist Painting 91

Another Drunken Phone Call 92

Free Minutes on a Cell Phone 93

The Dao of Being Dumped 94

Moving Day 95

The Real Tin Flower 96

The Intelligent Animal 97

Get Zen 98

Refusal to Mourn 99

He Had Some Sort of Demon Perched Upon His Shoulder 100

The New Math 101

Worn 102

Nathan Tells Him 103

Waiting for a Bus in Oakland 104

Notes on the Poems **105**

Acknowledgments

I would like to thank the community of writers and friends who helped me: Willis Barnstone, Aliki Barnstone, Stanley Moss, Caley O'Dwyer, Tom Babayan, Caroline Heldman, Christopher Bakken, Mark Turpin, Tim Fuller, and Alan Michael Parker. I also thank Richard Logsdon and William Baer for their enthusiasm and support. It is deeply appreciated. Thanks as well to the California Arts Council for a fellowship that gave me essential financial assistance during the writing of this book.

Poems from this book have appeared in the following journals, often in earlier forms and with alternate titles. Many thanks for permission to reprint them here.

The Drunken Boat: "In a Hotel in Portugal," "She Settled for Him," "His Younger Wife," "He Gets Up off the Floor," "Break Up with Him (A How-to Manual)," "Another Troy," "Antonyms," "What He Heard," "What Her Father Said," "Laughing Poem," "After She Sat Down on the Couch and Told Him the Marriage Was Done," "He Had to Leave on a Business Trip," "His Wheels Are Whining," "A Children's Tale," "Sad Jazz," "On a Blow-Up Bed in the Study of His Father's Apartment," "Cut Off," "Barbeque," "His Niece and Nephew on the Beach," "Waking Up Drunk," "A Cathedral in San Gimignano," "He Murders His Darlings," "Get Zen," "The New Math," "Worn," "Nathan Tells Him"; *Prairie Schooner:* "How to Live in This World"; *Faultline:* "Waiting for a Bus in Oakland"; *The Cipher Journal:* "Perhaps She Needed to Be Cruel to Make Him Understand," "Petrarch, Sonnet 195," "Petrarch, Sonnet 196"; *Nimrod:* "Marriage Psalm"; *The Red Rock Review:* "Dark Lord," "The Grave," "Nightmare Kiss," "The Orchid Creature," "The Happiest Man in the World"; *Margie:* "He Pays the Bill at the Sidewalk Café," "A Bowl of Bean Soup"; *The Formalist:* "The Audit," "The Bed Is Wide," "The Ghost Limb," "Moving Day"; *Timber Creek Review:* "He Goes to See the Doctor," "He Saw Her Car"; *The Well Tempered*

Sonnet: "He Wishes He Were Dead"; *Blue Moon Review:* "Aftermath"; *Valparaiso Poetry Review:* "Two Tickets"; *Rattle:* "The Truth Is that He Never Was that Good at Flirting, But His Friends Did Their Best to Set Him Up"; *Sonnets: 150 Contemporary Sonnets.* Edited by William Baer (University of Evansville Press, 2005): "The Audit," "Arithmetic."

The Bed

CXCVI
Petrarch

L'aura serena che fra verdi fronde
mormorando a ferir nel volto viemme
fammi risovenir quand'Amor diemme
le prime piaghe, sí dolci profonde;
e 'l bel viso veder, ch'altri m'asconde
che sdegno o gelosia celato tiemme;
et le chiome or avolte in perle e 'n gemme,
allora sciolte, et sovra or terso bionde:
le quali ella spargea sí dolcemente,
et raccogliea con sí leggiadri modi,
che ripensando anchor trema la mente;
torsele il tempo poi in piú saldi nodi,
et strinse 'l cor d'un laccio sí possente,
che Morte sola fia ch'indi lo snodi.

Sonnet 196

translated by Tony Barnstone

The tranquil aura winding through green leaves
comes murmuring then slaps me in the face
and makes me think of how it was that day
Love first inflicted wounds, so sweet and deep,
and makes me see the lovely face she holds
aloof, that jealousy or anger veils
from me, and her gold hair entwined with pearls
and gems, or blonde as newly polished gold
when with a toss she'd let her hair unwind
and then so charmingly restrain her locks
that thinking back on it still shakes my mind.
Then time entangled me inside those knots
and time tied my heart with a sturdy twine
that only Death will know the manner to unknot.

Marriage Psalm

Blessed is the mattress on which they feast.
Blessed the yellow sheet on which she lies,
blessed her skin and blessed are her breasts,
and blessed are the body's lamps, her eyes
lighting the room, rolling in dream, in lies,
and blessed is the darkness that descends
and carries them through sleep. Blessed the ways
of limbs entwined, a tangle without end
that only lack of love or death or time
can untie. Blessed mouth that eats the wool
pants and the folded sweaters, blessed blind
pink worm that digs, the insect in the wall
that feeds on them like rot in fruit yet gives
them years alive with blessings in their lives.

Dancing out of the Shower

It's one of the peculiarities
of this antic love that if in the blank haze
of dawn he sees her in a pool of sleep,
still glued into an armchair in a glaze
of morning light, he'll shuck his towel and wave
his Greek ass, chirping *ee! ee!,* a deranged
monkey, and though she has the right to rave
at him for being silly, crazy, strange,
she's likely (and in truth this is the reason
he loves her) to strip off her slip, embrace
his wet and pallid flesh and whirl him free
around the living room, tickling and teasing,
a pure hilarity lighting her face,
while singing out that morning song: *ee! ee!*

Kabbalah

Two eyes, one nose, one mouth, and what could be
more perfect? Maybe the small fraction of
a smile she aims at his glance secretly
across the table, kabbalistic love
that no one else divines, and later in
the loft their silent battle not to wake
her friend down on the couch, who snores as thin
strained cries rain down. Maybe the way they take
the root of self, forgetting *mine* and *yours*,
and add one body to another, blue
sensation multiplied, one, two and four,
arithmetic of love they do as years
subtract themselves yet strangely add up to
how much, how many, and to how much more.

It

He fell down to his knees, holding his head.
He didn't know what hit him when he stepped
through the low bathroom doorframe, but it clubbed
him into blackness as her nipples had,
pushing through the light blouse ten years ago,
crushing his eyes like grapes. Now he cried
and held his head to keep himself inside
himself, but he was out of his skull. Though
she screamed and put an icepack on his head
he'd left something behind that door, some knack
for being single. Plural now, they shop
together in the aisle of fruit. She hides
behind the oranges, then taps his butt,
yelling, *You're it!* She's it for him, too. But...

Falling Through

The smallest ticking of a clock. A soft-
ness they relax into like easing in
a bath, like water in the earth. A cough
of engines. Then, barely ringing in
the ear, a car's small whine begins to fade
down a far highway. Now there is no sound.
The town shuts down beyond the windowshade
as they slip through the sheets into the ground
and leak away where buried rivers flow.
As he descends he finds that he can't sense her
at the horizon of his body. Now
he's pulled by gravity down through a blur
where he takes fractions of himself and then
forgets to be until he is again.

In Her Dream He Touches Her Shoulder

The television squabbles lightly and
she moans and throws her knee against his back.
Her fingers crawl the sheet, seeking his hand.
He huddles in blue spray, insomniac.
He turns the TV off and sits a while,
watching the room shrink to a glowing ball.
He draws dream sharks, weird manta rays, a whale,
in dust on the blank glass but cannot fall
through sleep. When will a hand turn him off too?
Like Shakespeare's sailor turning in the sea,
he'll change, he'll meet her strangely in the flow.
He kisses her. Weakly her hand lifts to
his face. A cartoon shivers in her dream,
a small shock of *It's me.* And she says *Oh.*

In a Hotel in Portugal

The drywall was papyrus thin, so when
a bedspring creaked for the first time she cried
out a small shriek, thinking, *a bird* and then
the rhythmic squeaking on the other side,
and then the headboard banging on the wall,
and then his father's girlfriend called *O, O,*
little dove cries, little death cries, all while
they stifled laughs, naked themselves below
coarse sheets, and high on ecstacy, all in
those days when they shaved heads and started over
and spent a decade in the ocean's mouth,
four of them rolling in cheap hotel linen,
his head held in her palms until he found
with his tongue the dark honey at the center.

At Suicide Beach

The first year in his life of loving her
becomes a circle widening as if
a fat red onion's rings were sliced clear
to its round heart. They circle down the cliff
through a sand valley where ghost grasses reach
long salt fingers around the windfall limbs,
skidding down the loose scree to the beach.
They listen as each ocean wave slams in
and a bell-clapper sings against the shore,
sending waves ringing out to sea again
like blue breaths drawn into a darkening core.
How young they are, how stupid, sure that in
their lives their love can do nothing but swell
like breathing music, ocean cries, like bells.

How to Live in This World

The body's cup is broken into psalm
because a fever in the mind declares
there's nothing here but raw bones, gristle, hair,
nothing but living shaken out of song,
else nothing but the world and nothing else.
He breaks into her, breaks in her mouth, wrecks
the cup to free the clay, and breaks and breaks
in waves that follow other waves, and pulse.
Turn back from the door. Please. Do you love me?
He breathes into her neck and finds a summer.
What does it mean to have her without holding,
to hold her, not having to hold, and be
a mortal voice that sings below the water?
He feels that he can live in that unfolding.

(Written with Li-Young Lee)

12

Throwing Stones at the Beach

They swim away from the families
with striped umbrellas, from naked children
with pails being chased by young mothers
trying to pin a hat on a moving head,
the teenagers, all thin and tan and muscle,
lying in a circle around a boombox,
cheetahs around the corpse of a wildebeest.
They swim away, eyes open to a salt world,
and wash ashore in a cove where they
pick up round stones to throw into blue.
They throw them, opaque and clear,
green for career, white against cancer, translucent
blue for a house, and one dark yellow heart
to help a loved one wrestling with her rage.

And the Sea Takes Their Wishes

In the surf seaweed tosses and sand
and small stones grind their teeth.
They throw little green anxieties,
clean blue wishes, glistening in long arcs
towards the families playing at the edge
of the world. And the sea takes their wishes
inside its body to be cleaned and held
and chewed and beaten and cast ashore again.
And the sea speaks to them in soft voices
as they cut it, and the sea closes over its wounds.
And the sea opens itself and takes them in,
it takes in everything, sparkling, beautiful,
and in the end it eats them up, very, very gently
as they swim in its mouth back to shore.

Thing in the Mirror

Dark Lord

With a fast clenching of his black-gloved hand
Darth Vader squeezed off a man's windpipe for
doubting his force. The squirming captain tore
his throat as unseen fingers found him and
then he sat silent. Afterward, in bed,
she said, "It's funny seeing how *Star Wars*
is tacky now, the love story, death stars,
the quest resolved by the third act." He said
nothing, but watched the light as the light died,
and tried to see their future. It was obscured.
The dark side of the force, he thought, it's blurred
my sight! He almost laughed. Then the dark side
blotted the window, stained their lives, the moon
turned comical, and darkness crushed the room.

Insect Wings

Inside his dream, he watches her face close
like a blank envelope. She's opening
him up, as easy as tearing a wing
off a white flower. In this dream, who knows
the way to read the ocean speaking in
blue tongues, the apples ripe with a raw word,
and who can understand the yellow sting
of hornets, fumbling of the buses, weird
trailers with open mouths? In the blue night
he gapes, a fish, but when he wakes she's his
again, though as she curls into his hip
he feels dream fingernails tear this from that,
and with a certain cruelty looks at
mosquitoes lashing wings against the net.

Zombies

The coupling couple disengaged their limbs.
First he withdrew from her, then she drew back
as well, and lay by him, demi–detached.
His sperm inside her wept like honey, clotting
on the blue sheet. *Did you like that?* he asked.
Uh-huh, she said, her face turned to the pillow.
Now sitting naked at his desk, he tried
to write, but nothing seemed like anything
to him. The stubborn world refused to rhyme.
The glue was gone. The moon spun off to try
out outer space, and molecules gave up,
their complicated gravity set free.
I'm going now, she said. *Mmh-hmm,* he murmured,
studying the screen, and didn't hear her leave.

Thing in the Mirror

He couldn't peel the onion. The center
eluded him, the planet's heart. Each skin
he pulled off just revealed another skin,
skins within skins, more surfaces. He'd enter
her and dig in to find her spot. She'd wail,
he guessed, with pleasure, both hands on his chest
and riding him, eyes closed, then lie on chaste
blank sheets, filmed with his seed and watch the wall.
"I'm like a mirror," she told him, "My head
reflects my father, you, our friends, but can't
show what I am myself. Tell me, what's mine?"
And when he said "I love you," she just said,
"I've never chosen anything. I don't
know what I am, so what does your love mean?"

Nightmare Kiss

The middle of a kiss, and though he opened
up wide and wider, her own small jawbones gave
a little *crack* and stuck, and look what happened:
as if she'd fallen in an open grave,
he swallowed her at last, and then she wandered
in a dark saturated country where
the red land throbbed with capillaries under
electric stars. A kiss had brought her there,
a simple kiss that rained and filled her head
with blood, a nightmare kiss, a wrong man kiss;
why had she kissed a man with such a mouth,
with such thick teeth and jaws, such tongue, instead
of kissing someone who would let her out,
kissing someone nicer, who ate less.

20

The Grave

His gravest fear: he will be declared dead
and planted in the soil, and when unearthed
they'll find he's clawed the casket under earth,
his mobile features hardened to pure dread,
with fractured fingernails, on his rouged face
fresh stubble. Lying in the morgue, perhaps
he'll gasp and call and kick inside his nap,
yet still be thought dead (it's a commonplace
that gas can make a corpse grunt like a pig
and fart and moan while twisting like a vine).
He wakes his wife at night, buried in the covers,
mouth filling up with dirt when he cries *Why!*
She's learned to wait, to read till it is over,
until his numb arms stop trying to dig.

Spider Woman

It's hard to process if you have no drive,
when the cold brain transmits an error code,
some *file not found,* some *data overload.*
Without an integrated system, life
becomes a long down–time, a system scan
that goes for weeks and seeks the reason why
the network's crashed, corrupted code inside
somewhere, no one knows where, so the broadband
secure connection to the world goes dead
and she goes down and can't boot up, just lies
in bed in her pajamas, staring up
at cobwebs in the corner, and can't stop
her brain from spinning, spinning, spinning like
a spider given acid, a mad web.

Spider Man

He wants to grab a leg, a breast, an ass,
a muscled belly, a round hip, a foot,
a rope of hair descending from the roots,
a small blown kiss, with his eight hands, but has
no one to capture, sling up, drain dry, eat
but himself, so he starts to climb the wall,
poisons himself from some dark sac, some well
of bile, then feeds. He'd like to leave this meat,
wants to launch filament and filament
out of his body till one catches, clings,
but shoots into a void. He wants to swing
from his own cord, a dead lightbulb. She bent
his soul, then gave it back, and now he's feeling
stung like a webbed fly hanging from the ceiling.

The Orchid Creature

She's like an orchid in her bed of dirt,
just a root drinking silently, a mouth
that sucks and sucks at nothingness. Her shirt
is draped on the chair, bodiless, without
a thing to fill it up. She lies in bed
because without the drug she cannot stand
her mind. She's slack and empty. She has shed
her life and lives with naked nerves instead
of skin. She'd like a life. She lies beneath
a sheet and doesn't move. She's gone too deep.
She's like a creature sipping her own blood.
She's lost inside the tangle underneath.
She's like a body without soul. She sleeps.
She cannot stand herself. She lies in bed.

He Pays the Bill at the Sidewalk Café

She watches as he signals to the waiter.
He doesn't note how silent she is now,
he doesn't catch her sadness, can't see how
her eyes go dark and still as standing water.
Behind them in a fluid tangle, strange
ideas swim in black spirals, entwined
like eels. She watches how the subtle wind
tears at her husband's hat. It isn't strong
enough to toss it to the sky, but tugs
and grabs and shakes and doesn't stop. Perhaps
a hurricane is needed. What she hopes:
a bomb will drop, all things will die but bugs,
the continent will slip into the sea,
the planet will implode, and she'll be free.

The Happiest Man in the World

The Audit

The time has come he never thought would come
when he sees her see in him just defects.
As if his heavy love has kept her down,
what once she thought was perfect she rejects.
She takes an audit of his qualities,
subtracts affection, multiplies distress,
and so, in sum, she takes his sum and sees
the countless reasons she should need him less.
She knows him better than he knows himself
so if she finds his love to be oppression,
and reads all the good years as years of lies,
then he must turn his mind against himself
and see, laid out in infinite regression,
his net and gross of failure in her eyes.

The Happiest Man in the World

He curls up on the floor and thinks of dying.
He contemplates the ceiling, plans out ways:
the sudden swerve into the traffic pylons,
his new car crumpled like a beer can, glaze
of safety glass. But no, because he'd dive
into the airbags blossoming like stars,
like white-winged angels, and he would be saved
to suffer more, but now without a car.
Last week his friend told him, "You make me ill,
you're too damn happy." The next day his wife
said after thirteen years, "I don't think I
ever really loved you." He's thinking pills
now, but he has no pills. He can't think why
it is so hard to die. He stays alive.

He Gets Up off the Floor

That night he wanted alcohol and pills
but damn it, he had nothing, just some Tums,
some Advil, Bufferin, enough to kill
a headache or an acid twinge. Too dumb
to kill himself, he lived, and get this, now
she says, "You are the best thing in my life,"
and now she says, "I can't imagine how
I said those things." He'd like to trust his wife
but can't reply, and so grins anxiously.
He thinks about the windmill in his stomach,
constantly grinding him. Amazing, huh?
She asks him in the dark before they sleep,
"Who loves you?" Then she socks him in the stomach,
playfully, demandingly. With love.

She Settled for Him

She has her outbreaks when she tries to break
from him, but comes back, can't keep her resolve.
She steps outside herself to see herself,
dissatisfied, and glowering at her make-
up mirror doesn't see the beauty there
and so relents, and she becomes his wife
again, lives half her life, lives a half-life,
with him. There is a bubble filled with air
trapped in the glass. It magnifies, refracts,
and bends the light until the mirror lies
and shows only her flaws. Her mind of glass
distorts their love, their marriage. He maintains
she's like the Chinese poet who says, "I
can't see the mountain since I'm on the mountain."

His Younger Wife

They stayed together, and she said "I love
you" every hour, said "I don't want to leave,"
said "I would die for you, you are my life."
"Don't tell me that," he said, "I might believe
you." And he did. This was the year she wore
the little shirts cut off below the chest
to show the belly, tiny shorts, the wire
push-up bras to emphasize her breasts.
She wanted a tattoo and a pierced tongue
and navel. But piercing made him think of martyrs,
tattoos of plumbers and marines. His young
students did it to torment their fathers,
to hurt their pain. Yet what she said relieved
him; he believed at least that she believed.

They Had Terrific Sex

That week of fights they had terrific sex,
a rocking hip-hop jazz that made them numb
with ecstasy. They groaned more with the threat
each time might be the last, and they would come
to a new point where he was sitting on
the bed, erection pointing at the ceiling
enthusiastically, her easing down
the shaft, but carefully and slowly, saying
"Oh, just fuck me. Oh, that's hot." But in a while
the sex talk stops, she takes new pills, avoids
fighting with him, and feels relieved to state
"The doctor says the drug cuts back my drive,"
and not feel guilty held in his embrace,
his human teddy bear, just sleeping, void.

He Goes to See the Doctor

And later, when to piss began to hurt
and when the doctor raised his brow to say
"I don't want to say it's cancer, yet,"
she'd say "I love you" twenty times a day,
but then he felt too tired, balding, fat
to battle anymore. He thought, "Let me
go out with dignity, together, what-
ever, alone, but with some dignity."
And so it went: drawn blood, piss in a cup.
Later, he read infections make it seem
as if the groin were growing some dark thing,
sending out roots, and rushed to tell the doc,
who patted him with a cool tenderness
and murmured, "Let's just wait to see the tests."

After Eighteen Years

He thinks perhaps sometimes he is too crass.
Eyeing the slight smile of her hips, he grabs
her but she slips out of his clumsy grasp
like silk across a thigh and calls across
a shoulder, "Sorry, going out." The flesh
between his legs curves up like a hot knife
and radiates, but he's alone. His wife
seems not to want it anymore, to mesh
with him like thought and mind, like light and sky,
yet doesn't want to make suspicions rise
in his mind, minnows after bread crumbs, tries
to love, to keep her brain dark, tries to try.
She hides her cravings even from herself.
She shuts up like an oyster between shells.

What She Said

CXCV
Petrarch

Di dí in dí vo cangiando il viso e 'l pelo,
né però smorso i dolce inescati hami,
né sbranco i verdi et invescati rami
de l'arbor che né sol cura né gielo.
Senz'acqua il mare et senza stelle il cielo
fia inanzi ch'io non sempre tema et brami
la sua bell'ombra, et ch'i' non odi et ami
l'alta piaga amorosa, che mal celo.
Non spero del mio affanno aver mai posa,
infin ch'i' mi disosso et snervo et spolpo,
o la nemica mia pietà n'avesse.
Esser pò in'prima ogni impossibil cosa,
ch'altri che morte, od ella, sani 'l colpo
ch'Amor co' suoi belli occhi al cor m'impresse.

Sonnet 195

translated by Tony Barnstone

Relentlessly, my face and hair grow old
but still I need the hook and lure so sweet
and still can't let go of the evergreen,
the Laurel tree that scorns both sun and cold.
The sea will drain of water and the sky
of stars when I no longer dread and need
her gorgeous shadow; only then I'll cease
to hate and love love's wound I cannot hide.
I cannot hope to rest from breathless work
until I'm flayed, demuscled and deboned,
or till my nemesis will sympathize.
Though everything impossible occur,
still none but she or death can heal the wound
made in my heart with her amazing eyes.

Break Up with Him (A How-to Manual)

Score limbs and torso with a paring knife,
then peel just like a mango. If the skin
resists, to pry it up place a dull blade
beneath one edge and rock it back and forth.
With the meat flayed, it's easier to run
a slender blade between the muscles, then
to sever tendons and cut fat from flesh.
Now break the major joints with a steel hatchet,
crack bones as you would a lobster, crush
the skull with a small sledge and blend bone dust
with flesh. Wear plastic gloves, a heavy apron.
Then wait for turkey buzzards to wing in.
On clumsy chicken legs, with necks stretched out,
they will eat, watching you with burnished eyes.

Another Troy

Why should he blame her that she fills his days
with misery, like a curved hook inside
his belly he can't wriggle off, or why
should she blame him because he loves her face?
What made her simple as a flame that eats
the heart like kindling, eating it to live?
Why did he walk into the fire, give
his chest to the barbed shaft, and ask for peace?
Because embracing flame is still embrace,
because she needs another Troy to burn,
because she needs to crack his innocence
which keeps her chained to him and to this place.
From her small smile like a taut bow he learns
how much he needs even her violence.

The Hook

Look at how his face grows fat, and look,
his hair curls only like a sea around
an island of bald rock, and yet he's found
he still can't worm free from this hidden hook.
A subtle needle threads its way through him,
and stitches everything he does with pain.
Each time she says, "We need to talk," to him,
he sees the sun go blank, the oceans drain
into the toilet, planets rotting through.
He gnaws on every little thing she says
and feels the bones extracted from his flesh.
When she says, "I'd feel better without you,"
he feels his skin pulled off, his muscles flayed.
He needs her more the more she needs him less.

Antonyms

Although his love is on the incline,
she feels she just can't breathe, not here
with him, has to decline
this life and float somewhere,
to be away
where she can stay
forever,
one,
embracing never,
wanting no one.
She's chosen to retract
her love until his death.
He wishes she would give him back
his damage: half his life, each breath.

What She Said

"I must be very bad. But don't you see
it eating me, see why I have to go?
Of course I love you. You're too good for me."
Yet still not good enough? he asked. "Well, no."
She sipped at her café au lait. "I find
something is always biting at my mind.
It keeps chewing, no matter what I do.
I just can't see being with you forever,
having your kids, dying with you. I never
could completely give myself to you.
I've tried for all these years but I feel dead."
She took his sweaty hands in hers. "You know,
of course, I still would die for you," she said.
But would you still die without me? "Well, no."

What He Heard

He thinks he sees the space between her words,
the unknown underneath, can diagnose
the case, so he ignores the things he's heard
her say, the symptoms, postulates he knows
the concealed truth, and in this way resists,
playing good doctor in white coat and specs.
His precise methodology consists
of changing the results to match his ex-
pectations, treating cancers with hot glass
and distillations of cocaine and spirits
like a dense charlatan out of the past,
theosophist or vitalist, a fool.
The patient's dead. He doesn't have the tools
to understand. He doesn't want to hear it.

What He Tries Not to Say

He knows he has to hide his love for her.
She has withdrawn from him but still will see
him if he doesn't ask too much. The seed
is waiting underneath his words, interred,
internal, sending tendrils through his brain;
though they still meet as ghosts of who they were,
have sex, a movie maybe, there's a war
within him not to yowl and mewl in pain.
It tries escaping from his mouth but he
bites it off. When it trickles from his eyes,
he drops the lids. It burrows through his thighs;
he crosses legs. And then, when thankfully
it seems to stop, it tricks him: crossing legs,
and blind and mute, he can't stop it. He begs.

What Her Father Said

After the barbeque the men stayed out
in the cold garden drinking sake, rum,
and whiskey, stomachs warm and fingers numb.
The yellow cat began to nose about
the chicken bones and cold asparagus,
leftover steak and daikon radish, salt
soy beans, cucumber salad. "It's my fault,"
he said, "She doesn't want me." "Just give us
some time," her father said—his gray hair tied back—
gripped his son-in-law's hands across the table
and held them tight, tight. "Listen to me,"
he said, "In Japan, we say a dog is able
to eat all things, will even lick its ass.
But marriage trouble, even dogs won't eat."

Laughing Poem

He started laughing. But what kind of laugh?
A funeral black laugh. A bad joke laugh.
A cracked man laugh. He couldn't stop the laugh,
it came out of his mouth, a dead life laugh,
a dead love laugh, a laugh at faith, a laugh
at his sad, laughable self. What a laugh,
she said "Don't fight for me," and what a laugh,
she said "I'm tired of you," and what a laugh,
she said "Let me alone." That's when the laugh
erupted. What a joke, he thought, and laughed
again, a tight chest laugh, a heave, a laugh
from the odd clown, from the numb mind, a laugh
and then collapse onto the couch, a *ha*
all teeth and tears and gasping, *ah, ha, ha.*

Screw the Beatles

Screw the Beatles for singing "Love is all
you need," and screw him for believing them,
for thinking his love strong enough to stall
her doubts. It was, at times, but after time
had time to work, they bloomed like rumors. Damn
his faith that faith could even create god,
a god to bless their lives, who says "I am
in you," and damn the god that made love good.
Fuck him for not delighting her enough
and fuck him for being patient with her qualms.
Goddamn her for not knowing who she was
yet saying "I love you," while he wrote psalms
adoring her. Damn all the things she said.
And damn their love for being dead, dead, dead.

A Bowl of Bean Soup

"You don't know anything," he hears her snap
through the screen door, out on the patio,
smoking. She says, "Why can't he let me go?"
He holds a bowl of bean soup on his lap.
Back when his brother called, he'd said, "You talk,
I don't know how to tell him," and gave up
the phone and sat down with his soup. He shuts
his eyes and forces a few sips, then stops.
His stomach is too tight. Great soup, no meat,
three kinds of bean, white corn and carrots, but
he can't go on. To live you have to eat.
Why do you have to live? The beans are hot
and something tight inside begins to give.
One spoon. Another. This is how you live.

Driving Away From Her

Bad Drivers

The way he likes to think of it, he lives
on the black highway, tunneling through trees
like sponges soaking up the dusk, and drives
into the moon's bright headlight, darkly free.
He likes to think this way to indicate
he's not an accident but a joy ride,
that if he wanted he could find the brake
or he could swerve and find a hidden drive.
Whatever way he thinks, he is without
a choice when she tells him she wants another
model of man, to try another lover
before she gets too old and misses out.
She says, "I think this is a big mistake"
when they make love—then rides him till he breaks.

After She Sat Down on the Couch and Told Him
the Marriage Was Done

He drove away from her. He drove until
the city flattened in the mirror, crops
diminished in the chocolate fields, until
the sky turned zinc. He sped past the rest stops
and drove until the mountains tilted him
into null air. He saw a pile of tires
burning. A tufted owl dived straight at him,
then veered away. He almost crashed. Too tired
to drive, he drove into exhaustion. Death
was on the road and he aimed straight for it:
a zero time, a cobwebbed love, decay,
a world of dust and chalk, pathetic yet
where else to live? So he drove into it
and drove away from her, drove her away.

The Pits

He's driving past a sand pit, gravel pit,
with metal cranes, and piles and piles. Who knows
what kind of thing the open crane mouth gnaws?
Limestone, diamonds, what kind of pit is it?
How the hell is he supposed to guess?
He didn't know about the underneath,
the tumor growing like a fetus, death
beneath the skin, the way she loved him less
because of something hidden, her mind full
of dreams of other men. He sobs as wind
picks up and beats the car and stains his shirt
with tea. He swerves. This once was beautiful,
he thinks, this pit, this gouge, this earthly wound,
this pock, these rusting cranes, piles of raw dirt.

His Wheels Are Whining

He's driving on the freeway. Cows and grass,
the hills like naked bodies, the phone line
towers like Chinese characters, all pass
though glass and eyes and then are left behind.
Metal windmills turning like robot arms,
the barbed wire fences cutting up the fields
or stitching fields together (mend or harm
depends on how you see it). Now his wheels
are whining, now he's bellowing just like
an animal, he's screaming while he drives.
The windmills spin, the towers speak, he looks
at fences slicing what was joined: two lives.
He thinks he'd better pull off to the side.
He's driving, sobbing, trying not to die.

Suicide Road

The road is opening to open road
and tiny markers marking miles that pass.
A barn quivers with fire while the sun lasts.
Why must the world be so damn cute? The red
of clouds descending is becoming blue
and lead. At dusk the river turns to light
gray silk, and kamikaze insects fight
the windshield and get creamed. Why would she choose
to die? He thinks he is surviving death
by suicide, since she assumes that she
must die out of his life to live. Now he
is losing it and cannot catch his breath.
And here's the worst: she's made him understand.
Damn, damn, damn. God fucking damn.

He Saw Her Car

He saw her car on the freeway. It wasn't
her car. Inside, a Middle-Eastern man,
mustached and fat, was drinking from a can.
He saw her face across the room. It wasn't
her face that turned to him, returned his gaze
with large dark eyes, making him flinch away.
He saw her body on the beach. It wasn't
her body. It was someone else's pleasant
shoulders, slender and tan, taking in sun.
He heard her voice down the hallway. It wasn't
her voice. It was his brain, so full of wiles,
so full of hope, of loss, so full of it.
The car he saw was not her car, but
it followed him for miles and miles and miles.

Aftermath

A Children's Tale

He thought he knew the story of his life.
His story held sweet milk, rosemary, rings
of lemon, clustered fruit, and, of course, love.
His present held her body glistening
in the dark room with an internal light.
His past was hope like swinging bells that called
him to the temple, a light smile alight-
ing on her lips, then folding wings. And all
his futures, all of them lighted by her.
But like a children's story turning strange,
he now saw coats of thorns, wolves with necks wrung,
tarred fish and crippled angels, lizards, hair
torn out, and pins. Somehow the story changed,
his futures ever after all gone wrong.

Until She Left

He didn't dream about the end of dreams;
as life flew by he slept inside the flow
and didn't know how little he would know,
and didn't see his being turned to "seems"
until the water drained out of the lake,
until the pipes clogged up like clotting veins,
until the poems he wrote had lost their names,
until his heart had turned to bloody steak.
Now everything seems hyperbolic: skin
where sun breeds lesions, how the whole blue earth
(or just his stupid brain) is sick. She's gone;
he's ill. Now people edge away from him
at parties like he is infectious: breathe
out and divorce will sicken everyone.

Out, Out, Out

On the first day without her in his life
a zero blossoms at the core, a hole
in his mind echoing. A vacant laugh
is spreading rings of tumult through the whole
of him no longer whole, like a white blast
reverberating from ground zero and
whiting out the cities in its path.
He forms his mouth into an O and plans
to say something. Why bother? Words express
nothing. The hurt inside his gut comes out
as breath he plays with lips and tongue and mouth
like white noise from an air conditioner,
a fan articulating emptiness,
zeros multiplying his loss of her.

Zero at the Bone

And now she takes her chance and blows like wind
out through the door she's ripped out of his life.
And now his spirit clamps around the wound
and seizes up like flesh around a knife.
And now he feels an anger that could crush
the bones of planets, hates his worried face,
his roll of fat, the strands of hair his brush
picks from his scalp. And now she's gone. No force
can fetch her back like Lazarus from death.
She's in the undiscovered country where
she's free of him. And now there's only love
to love, invisible as God, as breath
siphoning from a hole. What's left of her
for him? An absence in which to believe.

The Bed Is Wide

The bed is wide. He turns and stretches out
a hand and touches no one, nothing there,
no soft horizon breathing dark, no hair
meandering through sheets into his mouth,
no breast, no dip above the hip, no skin.
The bed is infinite, it spreads into
a future full of nightsweat nights when through
the dark no hand is reaching out for him.
What comfort in this comforter, this stark
cold sack? The bed is wide and empty and
it has blank sheets to cover up the dead.
Its ghosts afflict the journey through the dark.
The bed is wide. He stretches out his hand.
He'll never reach the edges of this bed.

George Harrison Died around the Same Time His Marriage Did

He wakes up in the morning and he weeps
to hear a song play on the radio:
You're asking me will my love grow,
I don't know, I don't know. He knows. For weeks
he's woken up from dreams she loved him still
or simply that she smiled at him, and found
the truth to be his stupid, stupid mind,
the daze of stomachache and sleeping pills.
You know it don't come easy, and you know
the mornings are the worst, because at night
he's happy dreaming, till the dreaming dies.
And though he's not a weeper, never, now
he punches the snooze button, hits the light,
then realizes his brain has lied, and cries.

He Wishes He Were Dead

He saw her last night in a dream. She perched
before the mirror putting on her face
and smiled at his reflection. But no trace
lingers in air when he unsticks his parched
eyelids and groans and kicks the covers off.
She's vanished like the ancient dead beneath
the earth, preserved inside his mind in death
in a glass coffin. Animator of
the world, please let this toy run down, please make
him lifeless. Please. Why should he have to be?
To sleep, perchance to dream—that fantasy.
But just in sleep is there a hope she'll break
the mirror and wake him. Let him go cold.
Then she might smile. Missing her makes him old.

Sad Jazz

Inside his blue cocoon, cocoon of blues
on the couch under the down comforter,
he listens to sad jazz and thinks of her.
The first disc plays Miles Davis, "Kind of Blue,"
the way he feels. The ceiling is a blur
of whiteness spiderwebbed with earthquake cracks.
He's trying not to blame her, wants her back,
but listens to sad jazz and thinks of her
with someone else. When Bird comes on he sighs,
then listening to Parker play "Salt *Pea*nuts,
Salt *Pea*nuts," snarls a laugh and sings "sad *pe*nis,
sad *pe*nis" to the slack sack on his thigh.
He rides a borrowed couch, falls into blue
listening to the jazz die. He'd like to, too.

On a Blow-Up Bed in the Study of His Father's Apartment

Sleeping late. Now a car door slams outside
the window. *Damn* he moans and turns his head
into the pillow. No, no luck. The bed
can't carry him across the threshold, bride
of dreams again. Unbearable to be
awake, but pressure in his bladder, pain
below his shoulder blade, and in his brain
his father's cat is scratching, and his grief
won't let him sleep. He brushes eaten teeth,
gets his old body clean, hides it in clothes,
medicates the rot between his toes.
Now he looks almost good. But underneath
it all is melodrama. "Life is hell,"
he mumbles to the cat, "Life is hell."

Cut Off

She cuts him off the way she'd cut her hair and walk away
from the dead brown curls gathered in a circle round the chair.
She doesn't want to listen, she doesn't want to stay,
but still his mind is tangled by her wild black hair
that migrated through blankets in their old
bedroom into his mouth and hands. It's gone.
His hands grip air. What can he hold?
Her mole, her birthmark, trim arms, none
of them remain; she's cut
him off until it seems
there's nothing there
to embrace. But
he dreams
of hair.

Insects

He once read in a Japanese
memoir that you should never lift
up to your nose and sniff
young deer antlers, or seeth–
ing tiny insects,
a million specks,
will nest
infest
and eat your brain.
They are inside
worming behind his eyes.
The visions sting like brine
—the slight frown of her hips, her hair
tangled around his thoughts of her.

Wet Paper

The night is old, or maybe it's just him, writing at night
again, the sixty nights apart like sixty years alone.
He's sleeping on a borrowed bed, knows he can't phone
her up, she won't be there, not there for him. He writes
to understand this hole, and yet it chokes
him that he's starting to forget her laugh.
He can no longer read his life.
The page is wet and clean pen strokes
refuse to stay, to clot,
soaking across the white,
and in his brain
she is a blot
dark like
burst veins.

The Ghost Limb

Something was missing, something lost, a part
of him blown off in war, a ghostly limb
now gone, just an ellipsis. It made him
recall in Plato's genesis the start
of gender: man and woman once were one,
then cleaved and fated always to pursue
the missing half, a love to join onto.
So he had made a graft of her, fused bone
and brain, disease and sleep, and when she tore
herself from him was sure he couldn't live.
He found a way to be, how to survive
off balance, living with the gap, the tear,
the new white heat of amputated love,
yet always feeling the gone limb still there.

Barbeque

Berkel Berkel's Korean Barbeque:
the owner asks, "Where is your wife?" And he,
because the answer is too much, must do
his best not to flinch, hit himself, or scream.
He says, "She's well, she's with her parents now,
they own a restaurant and she's gone there
to help them out." But it is worse somehow
to lie with a straight face, shift in his chair
while his heart somersaults. His steaming brain
is a deep fry that cooks itself. Today
he orders beef bulkogi, kimchi, rice
and fresh bean sprouts, and then he eats his pain
and pays. "Give her my best," the owner says,
"She is so beautiful, such a good wife."

Aftermath

"How much do you love me," she teased him, "Tell."
He knew enough to count the ways he knows,
how rubbing slick and sticky aloe gel
on shoulders, neck, and down her collar bone
onto her breasts, he felt between his palms
the slender bones divided by the flesh,
the adding in of skin and scent like poems
of memory, oblivion and sex.
He counted on her. Why is he not angry
the day she cracks, and tells him to believe
she has to leave him gaping, leave him hungry,
that it's beyond all choice, she has to leave?
And she does, leaves him alone, leaves him flat,
and he still loves her. How much love is that?

End of the Vacation

Two Tickets

She leaves him just before their long-planned flight
to Europe, sticks him with two tickets he
cannot refund. "I could stay here and be
with you," he says. But, "No," she says, "don't fight
for me. I need you not to need me, need
not to need you." And so they pack their things
and drive out of Los Angeles. What stings
is her success in killing off her greed
for him, his body, jokes, his friendship, all
of him, unnecessary now. That's why
his absence makes her colder, why he bleats
into the phone and why she doesn't call
him back. She's gone, she's gone, and all the way
to Greece he sits next to an empty seat.

His Niece and Nephew on the Beach

He's standing naked, talking on a beach
below a small white church with a blue dome,
vacationing with family in Greece.
He is about eight thousand miles from home
and eating watermelon with Aní,
his topless friend from Portugal who says,
"I'd never guess. You were ideal to me,
you two." They watch as the small children play
with flippers in the surf, and then run up.
"Where is that girl, your wife?" his niece asks him.
"Shush, Maya," says her older brother, "We
aren't supposed to ask." "But where is she?"
she insists. "*Maya*, you have to shut up!
She doesn't like him now, so she stayed home."

Drinking Cuervo Gold with Andy, Joe and Roman and a Guy from Liverpool named Sven at Roman's Bar in Serifos, Greece

He floats into the bathroom, sees himself
soft-focus in the mirror. After ten
shots of tequila, things seem clear again,
at last. The vodka tonic didn't help,
and neither did the wine or the red drink
Roman made for him, called, he thinks, a spritz.
But now he's floating in the glass, adrift,
the yelling in his head subsides, the dank
bathroom is a hermitage where he's drunk
a magic potion and like a sad monk
can meditate upon the world and wait
to see what phantom will arise from that
mirage, that cesspool, next. He stares at
the toilet till the world dissolves in white.

Heart Sushi

He reached across the bar to grab a lime
and smeared it on the rim of the shot glass,
tossed back the shot and coughed. "One more time,
Roman! One more! Shots for my broken-ass
buddy!" his friend roared. Then, "You need to look
around. She's just one woman." "No, no more,
have pity on a ruined man. She tore
my heart out by the roots." "With a meat hook,"
his friend laughed. "Then she carved it up and served
it on a plate. She didn't even fry
it." "Yeah," he said. "Heart sushi. I deserved
it, trusting her. Some fool. I should just die."
His friend said, "Well, you are the man you are."
"Fuck me," he said, his head laid on the bar.

Waking Up Drunk

He wakes up drunk from ugly dreams. It's hot
outside and fifty flies have slipped in through
the door. He watches them whirl and corkscrew.
His stomach does the twist. With half a heart
he swats the busy air with a dry mop,
but they divide like water, then close in
again and pirouette and roll and spin.
So much for booze. It won't make his mind stop.
"My God this sucks," he slurs, and excavates
the mini fridge. Perhaps something in there
will make it better, coffee maybe, toast.
His mind does flips, but he grabs eggs and plates
and in the copper pan a dull face stares
at him from nether worlds, a thirsty ghost.

In These Old European Towns the Streets Wrap
Back upon Themselves Like an Insidious Argument

He walks into the labyrinth, the white
stone streets of this Greek mountain village, tangle
of tiny paths, each corner and new angle
of sight revealing marble tombs, the bright
blue domes of churches, children looking up
with mocking eyes, arched tunnels through thick walls
of the old fortress, covered marble wells
and fountains dug into the cliff to tap
the deep spring waters. Complicated knot
of streets, how can he solve it? There is no
young Alexander who with a sword blow
severed the Gordian knot, and so the net
that binds him spreads inside his head, his lust
for love, that maze. He walks until he's lost.

After the Night Swim

Gerard is telling stories naked on
the beach. A handsome graying chamer, smooth,
a hippie who's gone hip, he's happy nude
the way he was in a free time now gone
when he lived on this beach and tended bar
upon a rock below the cliff. Those days
were days of bonfires and of easy lays,
of poverty and youth, everyone bare,
elated, smoking hash. Now after many
vodkas, as meteorites illumine half
the sky, white streaks on a chalkboard, he tells
him, "Look, you grew up with your wife. But any
new woman will have lived already, have
a history. And history is hell."

Foxes

He's in the north of Greece, the pine tree heights
where *kleftes*, bandits of the resistance
outsmarted Nazis and the Ottomans
in mountain battles. In two days he sights
three foxes. The first runs out of the trees
then whips its slender body round and leaps
from sight—a red bush tail, some shaking leaves.
The next one's slanted eyes eye his. He keeps
a marble fox his wife gave him and named
his spirit animal. It won't help fix
a thing. She outfoxed him—yielded, then numbed
her heart and laid him out like the third fox,
stretched along a roadside gutter, its eyes
like clouded quartz and crawling with black flies.

In the Ghetto

High over the old streets of Orvietto
is not the moon, but the round lit church clock
against a heaven of black brick. Why talk
of Italy at all when his own ghetto
has walled him in his mind? He wears the star
that means he's been cast out to wander through
the world unloved, at least one half a Jew,
like Yeshua Mashiah. He's too far
away from her and all this beauty's wasted,
these hollow cobbled streets echoing with
his footsteps, cold water of mountain air.
He looks into a store front. He has tasted
paradise and apocalypse, a myth
that left him by this wine shop, squandering air.

Bright Surface Seen through a Train Window

He breathes in the old stink of cigarettes
in this decrepit train so tightly packed
the people sit on suitcases and sweat,
watching the glass where Italy spins past,
shaved hills and rolls of hay. Trees by the tracks
are radiant blurs. He's near the end, his trip
about done and the world's fresh out of tricks.
It can't distract him anymore. He's trapped
himself in this old car, is forced to watch
the surge of apparitions in this ghost
land he is gliding through, a world in flight,
some castle passing by (he can't tell which),
corroded factories and rails. He's lost,
dark rust eats him. Pain rubs the surface bright.

The Truth Is He Never Was Good at Flirting, But His Friends Did Their Best to Set Him Up

Patricia looks just like a movie star,
you know, the actress who's in *Bridget Jones,*
what's her name, the pretty one, and he stares
at her a bit too much, feeling his bones
ignite with lust or the Greek sun. A tiny
yellow missile darts from the sky of glass:
a bee that stings her where her white bikini
bottom arches round her lovely ass,
and Jacoline says someone must suck out
the poison fast or else the wound will swell.
He gets the job and sucks with modest ardor
while everybody laughs. Patricia pouts,
"It hurts. It isn't coming out," then smiles,
"I'm sorry, but you'll have to suck it harder."

A Cathedral in San Gimignano

Bright frescos in the candy cane cathedral
show the dead living, climbing out of caskets
and riding devils into hell. Long needles
pierce their white limbs, cut hands are piled in baskets,
a rat-faced demon rides a naked girl
and Satan munches on a pair of legs.
He loves her but to her he's dead and whirl-
ing through red hells. He'd like to live and begs
his mind to cease this loving, lights a votive
candle. The next day in the locomotive,
a woman brushes by him in the aisle.
She only touches him with breasts and hips
and as she walks away she turns and smiles.
Perhaps this flesh will save his soul: her lips.

End of the Vacation

The smell of disinfectant. Anxious lines
at banks of telephones and internet
stations. Will they connect, have mail, or not?
Does someone wait for them to call? At times
the weary Asian lady (chewing gum,
arms crossed) lets her glance skid across his face,
then looks away, focusing on blank space.
A toddler kicks the carry-on. A young
man sleeps, head on his girlfriend's breast, and dreams
nice dreams, damn him. How much did this trip cost?
One life. Guards scan the passengers for danger
but he won't seek her in the crowd. He's seen
it now, she's a bad ticket, luggage lost.
She'd rather slip by in the flow, a stranger.

Get Zen

He Murders His Darlings

He thought of William Faulkner who once said
"Murder your darlings," meaning be dead cold
when you rewrite. To live himself he killed
his children who had never lived. The dead
were one small boy awakening to life,
with Asian eyes, his father's nose and dark
intense black curly hair, a girl so smart,
alert and happy she could make you laugh
with just a glance. He murdered them inside
his mind, and burned the house they hadn't bought,
and quit the job he didn't get, took off
the ring of white and yellow gold that lied
to him about his wife and children. Now,
alone, he should be able to live. How?

Like a Man in a Cubist Painting

Tonight the fetal shell of dream is cracked.
He leaps from bed wild-eyed as if a ghost
has grabbed him by the legs, and stands there lost,
awake again. Each day alone is stacked
upon the others, building what? Bad dreams.
At night his spirit twines above his bed,
smoke from a dying wick, free from his head
for a few hours, and plays out fractured dramas
until a lightbulb kindles dawn and wakes
his heart of loving meat, his beehive brain.
In eggshell morning light his being breaks
and he leaks tears, but only a brief rain
before his coffee, fruit and yogurt. Then
he seals his mind, sits down and eats again.

Another Drunken Phone Call

His love is nothing like the sun.
She hates being inert, a moon
where light rebounds, a drooping bloom
dead without sun. But she's no one.
And what is he without her? Less.
Just some dolt drinking in a bar
and picking, picking at a scar
while dancers reel through nothingness
(but what the hell, the Cuervo Gold
tastes clean as angel spit). The fries
are cold, he has no heart for food.
Ravenous for her, feeling old,
he calls her up. And when he lies,
"I'm over you," she says, "Oh, good."

Free Minutes on a Cell Phone

"I set you free," he whispered to the phone,
and with that sentence sentenced himself, locked
into his words. "Don't worry, I'll be fine,"
he lied, "I'm free as well." He almost dropped
the phone. "Excuse me, sorry, just a sec."
His voice was off. "Hold on, there's something wrong
with the damn thing." Some animal nosed sacks
of garbage on the corner, large black rings
around its cagey eyes. He lay back on
a pickup truck hood, looked up to the moon,
bright eye of frozen milk, a dead-as-lime
planet, beautiful. "Hello? Are you gone?"
she asked. "You know, I'm watching a raccoon,"
he laughed. Then gently said, "I'm out of time."

The Dao of Being Dumped

"Be water. Let the loss slide off. The love
you hold is not the love that stays. Do not
call her. Be soft, unbroken. All things leave,
so don't grasp them." But when he bursts at night
out of parched dreams, his lungs aflame, full of
green sickness, scrabbling for throat spray which
they say will soothe, he's thirsty for her love
and feels such nothingness he mumbles, "Bitch!
I loved you." Dao tells him, "Pain warps you whole,
it twists you straight, it hollows you to make
you full, frays you to make you new." Like hell.
Now warped and brittle, hollowed out and frayed,
there is no mystery of mysteries,
no Way. He bitches, "Screw philosophies."

Moving Day

He piles her boxes in the courtyard under
a tarp, the bookshelves, microwave, spare phone,
and though his friends make clear they wonder
why he would help her move, he says, "It's fine.
I want to save her money, help her out."
And he does—helps her move out, feeling weight
tear at his muscles. Now he is without
her things. They are inside the truck, her freight,
then on the freeway, then in her new flat,
then gone. He's glad to ache in shoulder blades
and arms. It means that though she's left him flat,
left him behind like old footprints, he's made
a choice as well, to move her, remove her,
a choice to move past, not be moved by her.

The Real Tin Flower

The pewter leaves turn over in the wind,
exhibit tiny networks of pink veins.
His life with her is mulch. He doesn't find
he's thinking of her much, though secret pains
are underneath the skin like pulsing tendons,
a hammered bruise, his rented courage. Thin
joy sprouts from the dark rot like a strange tin
flower, alive, unreal, a bloom to tend on
the days he cannot see his life. Such hell.
If you can't find your life then you build one
from tin or straw or clay, go out, have fun,
have sex, have doubts, then try again, oh, well,
oh, well, oh hell, what grows from waste, from mulch?
He's trying not to think of her so much.

The Intelligent Animal

The short-haired puppy leaps at his bare arm
and gnaws at the wrist white as a cow bone.
He knows those tiny jagged teeth can't harm
him yet pulls back and grabs the loose skin on
the puppy's neck and shakes him playfully.
The puppy yelps in rapture and then tries
to twist his head back, biting happily
at the air. "Anyway," he says, "I cried
an awful lot, became an expert weeper."
"Oh yeah," Kim says, "me too. Expert. Why not
be like an animal, play dumb and live
happy? At first, I wanted just to see her."
She hugs the puppy. "Once she left I got
him. I just felt I needed some pure love."

Get Zen

Get Zen, he thinks. Or try. Forget your lusts.
Think of that joke: What do you say to the man
who sells dogs at the Buddhist hotdog stand?
"Make me one with everything." He adjusts
himself upon the couch, stares at the dead
TV and tries. He tries to be remote
as the remote control, not to emit
emotion, thinks of what the Buddha said:
"The world is flame, a burning house where poor
people incinerate themselves among
the demons, wolves and vultures. Walk out." Young
last time he was alone, he just enjoyed
the show, the breasts and drugs like blazing toys,
but now he's old. Is there really a door?

Refusal to Mourn

Had he but world enough and time
he would mourn all their futures dead
till sci-fi empires failed. What crime
is it to give up, live instead
of rolling up into a ball
under the blue down comforter,
a maggot in a casket? All
he has of time is without her
jumping into his arms to ride
his waist when he walks in the door,
so let him stand up, walk outside
and through the iron gate before
the lid bangs shut, before he finds
he's laid inside the coffin, blind.

He Had Some Sort of Demon Perched Upon His Shoulder

He loved her but because his death was riding on his shoulder,
because it seemed to whisper like a demon in his ear
about his cracking knees and lower back, the years
that fall like hairs and leave the mirror looking older,
because of plaque constricting his blue veins,
and finally because you live and then
you don't, he tried to breathe again,
allowed himself to swallow pain.
Although the years ahead
seemed thin without his wife,
he wasn't dead—
not yet—would live
his life
alive.

The New Math

He's swimming at the public pool, his brain
filled with the mathematics of divorce,
how many months alone, how much new brawn
he's grown through savage discipline and force
of his despair, how slender is his waist
these days, how many years he financed her,
how much it stings, the eighteen years of waste
in love with her, how long he'll still have hair.
Problem: her passion didn't equal his.
Solution: what if she subtracted him?
Then he would have a choice: be some guy who's
pathetic, zero, or start a life. Grim,
ignoring a bone scraping in his knee,
he crawls hand over hand, counts one, two, three.

Worn

He's cleaning out the trunk in which his clothes
are stored for summer, bathing suits, surf shorts,
swimming goggles, neatly folded beach shirts,
all laundered, put in plastic, and then closed
away—and finds a black and silky bra,
some short shorts with a tiny waist, a sleek
black top, all empty of her, as is he,
although she ghosts through him all night and gnaws
his dreams. They were so close he thought he wore
her like a skin, as she wore him till they
wore out. When doubt crawled in, she stored away
her love and latched the trunk and left. It seems
he catches just a whiff of her somewhere
in the blouse. No, it's clean. Too clean, too clean.

Nathan Tells Him

He can't endure the grief and so he gives
in, goes on a blind date. He's always been
the kind to dive right in. But "Look, don't bone
her just because you can," says Nathan. "Have
respect. Respect yourself, respect disease.
It's plague time out there now." So he buys wine,
Italian cheeses, raspberries, and when
she comes by they just talk, walk at their ease,
and eat. Sure, it is like an interview
and sure he blows it. When you date, do not
go on about medieval empires. But
it's fine. He's doesn't want a wedding vow.
He doesn't want to sleep with her tonight
(does he?) As Nathan says, "Don't be a slut."

Waiting for a Bus in Oakland

That time of day when all things thicken, street-
corner honeyed with late afternoon glaze,
everything pastel and hushed, discreet.
And now a woman asks him for some change,
he gives her some, but wants to ask "Does any-
thing really ever change?" Just an old joke
he can't quite say while searching through his pennies.
Of course it does. One day the world is broken.
Then hot hurt cools to watercolor on
a day when palm trees shiver and dissolve
and sunlight blows through their high frazzled fronds.
A newspaper takes flight and then revolves.
A helicopter chops the sky. Stand up.
It's time. Begin to live. Here comes the bus.

Notes on the Poems:

In the poem "In the Ghetto," "Yeshua Mashiah" is the Hebrew name of Jesus Christ. A number of the sonnets in this book were inspired by other poets: the shaped poems by George Herbert's "Easter Wings"; "Another Drunken Phone Call," by Shakespeare's Sonnet 130; "The Audit" by Shakespeare, Sonnet 49; "Perhaps She Needed to Be Cruel to Make Him Understand" by Petrarch, Sonnet 195; "Another Troy" by William Butler Yeats' "No Second Troy"; "Spiderman" by Walt Whitman's "To A Noiseless Patient Spider"; "Refusal to Mourn" by Andrew Marvell's "To His Coy Mistress"; "The Real Tin Flower" by the poem of that name by Aliki Barnstone; "Cut Off" and "Insects" by Yosano Akiko's "Tangled Hair" tanka sequence. A variation of the title "He Murders His Darlings" has been attributed to Mark Twain, G. K. Chesterton, William Faulkner, and various other authors.